# Retaining American Individualism

# In A Control-Filled World!

The 2015 Edition

By Don Floyd

Copyright—All Rights Reserved

Neither the author nor the publisher shall have any liability to any person or entity with respect to any loss or damage caused or alleged to be caused directly or indirectly by the information contained in this book. This book neither offers nor suggests any medical or professional psychological advice. Readers accept responsibility for how they use the information or the philosophical concepts contained within this book. They therefore hereby release the author and publisher from any liability.

All rights reserved. No part of this book may be specifically reproduced in any form or by any electronic or mechanical means, including information storage and retrieval systems, without written permission from the author.

Copyright © 2014—Don Floyd, All Rights Reserved ISBN: 978-0-615-99976-0

DEDICATION

To all Americans who believe in the sovereignty of the individual and in the American spirit!

## About the Author

Don grew up in the greater Detroit area. His parents owned and ran a small family retail business in Detroit. Don holds a degree in educational psychology and he minored in evolutionary psychology at Wayne State University in Detroit.

Don participated in a pilot program geared to increase teacher effectiveness while he worked in cooperation with Wayne County Intermediate Schools and Title I. He postponed completion of his postgraduate degree in order to pursue this work and then went on to become a behavior specialist and learning consultant.

Don is also a Michigan certified K–8 teacher who served as a behavioral consultant working closely with school administrators. Additionally, he worked as a public school special education teacher, and is Michigan-certified in eight special education categories. He later worked as a consultant for an educational software company.

After working in the educational field, Don devoted many years focused on his independent behavioral research which consisted of the study of non-biological unlearned influences and the relationship between the human behavior and human nature.

## TABLE OF CONTENTS

**Introduction**

**Chapter 1**—The Theory of Contemporary Human Nature

**Chapter 2**—The Two Basic Mindsets

**Chapter 3**—Ratting Out the Truth about Spirit

**Chapter 4**—Control: On Track to Rule the Human Race

**Chapter 5**—America Goes from Protecting Its Citizens to Owning Its Citizens

**Conclusion**

**The Bill Of Rights**

## INTRODUCTION

This book is about how Americans can retain their individualism in a control-filled world. It examines the phenomenon of metaphysical selfish control, which is the need to control just for the sake of control.

The idea that there is an invisible, influential controlling force in the world is nothing new; what is new is that this book gives a name to this force and explains it in great detail. We call this force contemporary human nature. Contemporary human nature is part of an influential complex composed of calculating influences; a network that has the ability to deliver influences into people's consciousness. It uses group-think narratives and polarizing contexts. It communicates in the language of imagery in order to use its powerful, persuasive influences to govern and manage people in accordance with its agenda. It is anti-individual and obsessed with creating a fictitious reality; one that brings the world closer to a equality-for-all utopian society. Plus, it is also intent on conquering America! Its entire motivation is to acquire control.

Contemporary human nature (CHN) operates silently, using its power to convey deceptive imagery and present polarizing storylines. Its strategy includes manipulating perceptions and creating fake intuitive group ideas for the purpose of gaining control for itself.

CHN seeks to gain control for its own ends only, no matter what the final results may be. It does this by using its intuitive power to snatch individual energy, restricting choice, and enforcing conformity. It is on a mission to destroy ethical individualism and ruin America by turning it into a poor, equality-for-all utopia nation. As a result, America is losing its essential traditional ideals. But we need not let this force win!

This book was written to help put the individual theme back into the American purview. It shows how America's salvation depends upon citizens using their human qualities, such as thoughtfulness, entrepreneurism, individualism, foresight, empathy and the ethical expression of free will. These are the very things that contemporary human nature cannot comprehend, because it seeks only to control for the sake of control. It is a relentless group sociological spirit.

CHN has a chokehold on prosperity, individualism, and the American way. This is the perfect book to help you understand how to transcend the limitations imposed by CHN. It can help restore some valuable American principles, reinforce the idea of liberty and help put vitality back into America. Furthermore, this book can act as a desirable counterbalance to the powerful dominance of contemporary human nature's influence in America.

## CHAPTER ONE

## THE THEORY OF CONTEMPORARY HUMAN NATURE

Welcome to an excursion into the realm of metaphysical influences. During the course of this book, I will discuss a particular brand of human nature that I call contemporary human nature. Let's first begin with a brief look at basic human nature.

For hundreds of thousands of years throughout the very early stages of human existence, human nature benefited from a tribal-based force that maintained group cooperation. However, that raw human nature force may have outlived much of its usefulness as humans evolved into autonomous beings and that original human nature may have diminished into being something similar to what is commonly referred to as the collective consciousness. An invisible ubiquitous force that creates a mass hypnosis in humans.

The collective consciousness and the concept of the universal mind were ideas popularized in the late 1800s. They described a group-oriented third-party metaphysical force that directs influences into the consciousness in order to reinforce a particular social order. What we discuss in this book is an acute form of the collective consciousness, a form we call contemporary human nature (CHN). Like the collective consciousness, it contains a strong social cohesiveness. Unlike the collective consciousness, I found CHN to be a particular influential force that uses a scripted formula along with self-serving consciousness-altering tactics, all of which are dedicated to the creation of an equality-for-all utopian society.

CHN appears to act as an intuitive influential force. It is quite active and destructive to both independent humans and Western civilization. It is manipulative, deceptive and apparently it produces compelling solidarity messages that are intended to govern and manage humans into acting in anti-American and anti-individual ways.

CHN also apparently uses tactics in order to protect its control turf. Those tactics include creating false inner narratives, refashioning sentiments, advancing fictitious beliefs, planting self-serving motivations and exploiting emotions.

We speculate that CHN first got its footing in the human composite by dividing people into conflicting groups and using a divide- and-conquer strategy. It continues to work basically the same way. It also specializes in sending polarizing imagery into the consciousness in order to facilitate group divisiveness, and then it obtains more control by fostering animosities between groups. It also works to prevent individuals from acting on their own best interest. Its mission is to establish an equality-for-all utopian society for the purpose of controlling people.

CHN apparently operates on a preconscious level using visceral, image-sensitive inner communications in order to steer thoughts and feelings. Among other things, it lacks common sense and lacks the ability to think-ahead. It is process oriented with an unwavering ambition to achieve one result: an equality-for-all utopian society.

It appears to have already achieved one of its biggest anti-American goals: to downgrade self-reliance as being one of America's premiere underlying ideals. Without a fundamentally self-reliant citizenry, the American public is at the mercy of contemporary human nature and its control.

It also appears that CHN is on another major control-oriented mission in America, to force everyone into a poverty-stricken, equality-for-all conforming existence.

Contemporary human nature's goal is to establish a totally needy society for the purpose of gaining more control. Once a general state of equality-for-all is established, it will then enforce it, maintain it, and regulate it. An equality-for-all utopian America is also a veritable control bonanza for CHN. The problem is that the equality-for-all goal is only an illusionary goal.

CHN is a force that is basically immature, yet strategically calculating. Although its power is mostly illusory, it is still capable of deceiving people as it steals their individual control. Plus, it often has the power to put people's jobs, grades, or relationships in jeopardy, thereby adding to its controlling leverage.

Additionally, it presents its influences using a false aura of sincerity and a phony pretense of good intentions to assist its power. However, people are duped by it and believe its self-serving message. They become its victim and don't realize they have been misled until it is too late.

Apparently, CHN does not communicate in literal words. Instead, it communicates on a non-verbal level; an imagery level. People buy into it because people are not accustomed to dealing with that kind of persuasive messaging that has the power to attach punitive storylines to non-cooperative individuals; storylines that can pressure those individuals and make them appear as evil outcasts. It also creates peer pressure that collectively lead people into taking the path of least resistance, even when that path is obviously destructive.

Throughout this book we will examine some of the ways contemporary human nature undermines individual freedom while it aggressively proceeds to fulfill its quest for an equality-for-all utopian goal; feeding its need for control as it railroads the domain of the individual.

The idea that there is an active cunning self-serving invisible third-party force working against our free-will is a first step to defeating it.

**CHAPTER TWO**

THE TWO BASIC MINDSETS

As I continued to study CHN, increasingly I noticed the different ways in which it controlled people. It appeared to work by dividing people into groups, each with very different ways of seeing things. One group was particularly focused on categorizing people, labeling people and stereotyping. That group tended to see people in terms of generalizations, characterizations, impressions, imagery, and symbolism. It also projects fictitious realities that exploit fears and insecurities in order to make people conform to a illusionary group standard. We shall call that group of thinkers the contemporary human nature mindset group.

Furthermore, the contemporary human nature mindset group is also weak and it readily buys into all the deceptive techniques that CHN dishes out. Those techniques include intimidation, fear exploitation, and a variety of contrived influences; all presented to redirect people's focus of attention and manipulate them into an equality-for-all point of view. People with the contemporary human nature mindset have the power to resist the suggestive encouragements of CHN but they are not aware that they have that power.

However, there was another kind of mindset that was more independently oriented and more representational of people who see life in terms of actuality, not in terms of figurative generalizations. It was a mindset that was not obsessed with comparing and grouping people, and it was reflective of an ideology that I have always been raised with. I always thought of this mindset as one that represents American individualism; therefore, we will simply refer to this second mindset we mention as the American mindset. We shall talk a lot about the way I see this American mindset.

This American mindset relates to the traditional American view of life. It sees America as an opportunity-based nation built upon freedom of the individual. It wants all Americans to enjoy life regardless of their religion. Furthermore, it knows that civility does not rely on religion because it understands that basic law-abiding cooperation is important for everyone's sake, and it does not need religion to tell them that. Many Americans believe in religion and many others do not. In any case, one can sincerely believe in America as a constitutional nation and profoundly respect the right for anyone to practice religious freedom and fulfill their individual conscious.

This American mindset also admires ethical individualism and understands that laws need to be obeyed. It is also a mindset that reacts more to the character content of individuals, not to the color of their skin. The same ideal that MLK once famously supported.

Additionally, it accepts America's capitalist, free-market economic system and understands that the economy is much more profound than just being about money. Good-will, charity and helping those in need is also a bedrock trait of the true American mindset.

It also sees America's capitalistic free-market economy as being something that provides Americans with a wealth of choices from competition. That includes the choice to own or trade property; and the choice to gainfully profit from that system. It accepts the basic business model (and the profit motive) as being a key component of America's economy, and it understands America's business sector is ultimately responsible for both the quality of life of citizens and the vitality of the nation. The American mindset sees economic freedom as something not just about buying a big house with a built-in swimming pool; it sees economic freedom as something that directly and indirectly broadens opportunities for those who wish to be gainfully employed. Plus, it understands the link that exists between public safety, proper taxation and middle-class quality of life, when American society is filled with productive incentive-motivated individuals each exercising economic liberty in their own ways. Furthermore, it sees economic freedom as something necessary to prepare for one's retirement, help provide working capital to others or help make a better life for their children.

The American mindset believes in law-abiding self-regulation. It is not preoccupied with micromanaging fairness because it knows someone else will always have a louder voice, a luckier break, or an edge that will be used for that person's own advantage. Someone will always have some genetic difference or some family upbringing that cannot be compensated for, and knows the idea of providing others' with an absolute equal opportunity in life will therefore always be largely an illusion. No system can be truly fair for everyone. America is subjective because it has a systemic fairness that is based on individual effort and individual behavior.

Still another aspect of the American mindset is that it recognizes the importance of the concept of self-reliance and considers the work ethic a healthy social priority. It also sees personal responsibility and concern for family as two qualities that trump the idea of group equality.

Let's now look at still another very different mindset for the purpose of creating a contrast. It is one some people unfortunately have.

Some people approach their life like an actor from the 1950s apparently did. His name was James Dean. He died young while driving his Porsche incredibly recklessly. Police and experts at the site of the fatal crash claimed his car "accident" looked more like a suicide.

James Dean, like some other hard living young adults, seems to believe that life is a place to live fast and die young. They don't plan on living to a ripe old age and don't try hard to work towards long-term goals.

On the other hand, the American mindset believes life is a temporary special gift that warrants lifelong participation and years of earning life's rewards. Unlike the reckless, devil-may-care, and short-lived life of James Dean, those with the American mindset want to live a long worthwhile life. They also desire to be agents of goodwill and progress, and often try to leave behind a positive legacy.

Another feature of the American mindset is that it confidently recognizes that it has the real authority when it comes to control over its host. It knows when to challenge the force of CHN because it knows that there is no good alternative. It knows that allowing CHN to win is to sacrifice of one's humanity, and that is unacceptable. It also knows it must take an active role to stop it.

In the next chapter we will look at another interesting aspect of contemporary human nature and explore how it cunningly works to stifle individualism. We will also disclose more about its secret agenda, and discuss how we as individuals can protect ourselves from becoming its victim.

## CHAPTER THREE

### RATTING OUT THE TRUTH ABOUT SPIRIT!

In this chapter let us explore a particularly devious way in-which CHN works to thwart ethical individualism. It neutralizes and stifles a crucial part of our individual self: the spirit.

Our spirit is the ultimate determinant of behavior, optimism, and happiness. It acts as a motivational furnace to our being. Although it is often overlooked and underappreciated, yet intrinsic to our individual beings. It is also a human component that is essential to the health of America.

The nation of America began with a spirited quest for liberty that transformed undisciplined, untrained colonists into a determined band of citizen soldiers willing to risk a fight with what was, to that date, perhaps the world's most experienced and powerful military. They even risked the very real possibility of death by hanging. That alone helps to make the spirit-for-liberty a predominant American trait. As important as it is, the spirit-for-liberty often stays hidden and does not show itself until it is significantly tested.

Back when I was a psychology undergraduate, we studied B. F. Skinner's contributions to the world of behaviorism, which included the infamous operant conditioning chamber popularly known as the Skinner box. This was a big cage that offered small animals the opportunity to earn food in return for their work. Lab rats, for example, were required to work for their food by engaging in a particular on-task behavior: pressing a lever a certain number of times to receive positive reinforcement, often a cheese pellet. After the rat learned that pressing the lever a certain number of times would earn it food, it would then typically become a well-fed and compliant worker. Apparently the rat developed an inner sense of recognition of the amount of effort necessary to earn food.

The experimenter sometimes would change the work-reward requirement in order to gather fresh data. However, when the work-reward requirement for success was ramped up too much, the rat would demonstrate a phenomenon known as straining the work-behavior ratio. In other words, it would simply stop working when it got to a point where it felt that no amount of work would bring forth a desirable result. The rat didn't actually pass out or suffer extreme exhaustion. It still had ready access to water. The rat quit working for other than physical reasons. What happened could be described as the rat losing its motivation because the amount of work necessary was overly taxing.

I found this rat behavior interesting because it exposed the fact that when it comes to motivation, there is something more relevant involved than just the material reinforcement of food and water. The truth was, and still is, that the real essence of that lab-rat study was not about lab rats, food, or work; rather, it was really about spirit. When we examine spirit more closely, we will come to see how the spirit in humans is not entirely different from the spirit in a lab rat!

We spoke of the American spirit-for-liberty when it came to creating a nation. We can once again see that spirit-for-liberty in action when it came to America's stunning World War II victories.

Many think war is just about violence, death and destruction. However, America's victories over Japan and Germany may have been just as much about spirit and liberty.

We have also spoken about spirit, but now let's focus a bit on another American essential; liberty. However, unlike spirit, liberty is more complex. That is because there are two kinds of liberty. There is the spirit-for-liberty that we spoke of, and there is liberty itself.

World War II demonstrated how America contains both of those two different kinds of liberty. Although they may seem the same, liberty and the spirit-for-liberty are two very different things. We can look at America during World War II to see that difference more clearly.

It was liberty itself that provided America with the know-how to manufacture extraordinary quantities of war-related materials. It was that liberty that facilitated the learned know-how America needed to establish its necessary military product assembly-delivery chains, each with enormous output capabilities. That kind of know-how was developed as the result of generations of Americans growing up and working in a combination of liberty and capitalism, and that environment provided Americans with their uncanny knack for progressive innovation, the kind of innovative skill that was used to their military advantage. It was living in the combination of liberty and capitalism that gave Americans the ability to adapt its manufacturing plants, refit its factories, and convert them into efficient weaponry-manufacturing powerhouses. Compared to its enemies, America produced vastly superior amounts of military supplies and equipment, including planes, boats, and tanks. More specifically, it was economic liberty that made all that possible. Economic freedom also provides a source for taxes that pay for public safety, national defense and public services.

On the other hand, in the case of World War II the spirit-for-liberty supplied something else extremely valuable. The spirit-for liberty took the form of active human capital. That can be evidenced by the willing participation of hundreds of thousands of gutsy fighting soldiers, coupled with a robust supportive unified American public willing to put their all into winning both wars.

Although the spirit-for-liberty and liberty are different, together they both helped America, the underdog win two wars within a four-year period. They each helped win the wars in their own unique way, yet neither is acknowledged for being the powerful essential force they really are!

## Contemporary Human Nature Tries to Destroy Spirit

Unfortunately, spirit can succumb to contemporary human nature's influences because CHN slants the way life is perceived. It causes people to see themselves as powerless victims. It also causes them to lack the spirit for challenge and lack individual grit.

A strong spirit helps us endure life's setbacks. Ironically, it is the setbacks in life that are essential to stimulating determination and provoking innovation. Setbacks are really life's way of presenting us with new opportunities. The American mindset uses setbacks as necessary components and stepping-stones to growth and progress. It sees failures as motivational features that stimulate future successes.

For example, Israel views and treats individual entrepreneurs and start-up companies as if they are valuable cultural components, and that is what helped make little Israel a global leader in many different ways.

CHN undermines the courage to progress and it diminishes spirit. It encourages the perception that life is only a linear experience that operates within a static world. That, in turn, prevents people from appreciating one of the most valuable parts of who they are: their essential progressive selves. As we saw with the lab rat when it had no hope of earning a reward, people also can just stop trying when their spirit loses its zest. Their natural American hunger for entrepreneurial adventurism, individual advancement and desire to conquer challenges are also dampened. They fear taking chances and sedentary living take the place of aspiration and individual drive.

## The Zero-Sum-Game View of Life

A term commonly heard in the social sciences, especially within the field of community psychology, is zero-sum game. This refers to the kind of thinking that is much like the stifling kind of thinking we have just been discussing.

Zero-sum-game thinking believes that for every good side to something there is also an equally bad side. That for every win someone else has to lose. For example, it persuades people that every time a business executive scores a lucrative contract, somebody somewhere will consequently take a hit, or, that everything one uses automatically results in that much less for someone else, or, that one person's financial success causes someone else's poverty. Plus, it exclusively focuses just on outcomes as a judgmental metric, instead of considering other important contributing factors. That is linear thinking.

CHN emphasizes that linear-perception aspect of life, an aspect that is blind to the dynamic element of life. With the help of its powerful anti-individual influence, people become accustomed to thinking in these limited, single-dimensional terms. Sadly, this kind of diminished thinking lacks respect and appreciation for the magic that exists in the kinetic nature of life.

Another way to exemplify zero-sum-game thinking is to briefly examine some popular games. First, let's look at games that focus only on beating your opponent, including such classic games as Monopoly and musical chairs. These are games that emphasize outcome and winning. However, there are many different kinds of games. Scrabble-like games do not rely upon a conventional zero-sum-game format.

In Scrabble, for example, while there may be a limit to the total number of tiles, there is no limit to the number of points each player can earn. Additionally, one person does not lose points just because another gains them. Each player can earn points without anyone losing anything and without taking earned points away from an opponent. Although there is still only one ultimate winner, it's the actual playing of the game that is the most satisfying part, not the winning. Each player has fun by trying to accumulate as many points as possible. Plus, the excitement of the game is in the challenge of creating interesting word formations and practicing shrewdness. Those are the best rewards.

Scrabble-like games are liberation-oriented games because they do not restrict the players by only focusing on win–lose. Instead, they unleash creativity, fun, and spirit in the very process of playing them.

The reason this game comparison is relevant to the way we see life is because game formats have a certain similarity to our outlooks on life. In a sense, one can compare the Scrabble-like game format to the fundamental American landscape that we touched on earlier in this chapter.

America contains a landscape of liberty mixed with free-market capitalism. It is that very landscape that provides a fertile resource for self-improving possibilities, and it offers-up a variety of different arenas that can be utilized in rewarding ways. It also offers life an additional element in the form of individual adventure that challenges us and gives life more purpose, more choices and more available opportunities to work towards a better life. Furthermore, it supplies us with an array of exploratory channels which can be adapted to express our own brand of individual boldness, and individual forward moving boldness is part of the American mindset.

America presents its citizens with a valuable abundant, broad, freedom-based field for the American mindset to socialize or to profit, innovate, learn from or be creative. It is a field for people to be enterprising, expressive, goal oriented and productive. That is the very same field that produced the human skills and quality products necessary to send men to the moon and bring them safely back to Earth in 1969.

The American mindset also utilizes America's vast resource-filled landscape to create opportunity and to arrange or rearrange their individual lives in ways that make their lives work best. It allows citizens to try special things or to create their own version of the American dream. To accomplish things that go way beyond the simple context of win-lose.

Liberty in its raw form is absent of regulation. It is the freedom to self-express, exercise and self-direct our free-will as autonomous beings. To succeed, grow riches or fail and lose wealth. It also means the freedom to attain a position to help others, and at times need some help ourselves.

The American mindset has the potential to see past the cardboard life presented by CHN, and has the ability to focus on the fluid aspects of life. It senses beyond the cubical thinking that we have come to understand as the zero-sum-game platform, and is capable of moving its host forward even in the absence of certainty.

When I was attending middle school in Detroit, my ninth-grade science teacher made a remark that helps illustrate the nature of liberty. He said, "Darkness is the absence of light." This was such an unexpected and abstract fact for a youngster to comprehend, I still remember it. It amazed me that an entire realm of life can be uncovered only through the absence of something else. Liberty works the same way. Liberty can only exist in the absence of encroachment.

In time I learned how encroachments can hamper liberty in two different ways. They can come from the outside or they can be created on the inside due to a person's mindset. In other words, liberty is not always only about the absence of outside interference, it is also about one's inner perspective.

I also began to notice how some people unintentionally place self-imposing limits into their life by seeing life in restrictive or inhibiting terms. Even worse, I further saw how some people become obsessed with having to prove that failure is inevitable, instead of using their time and energy towards trying to create their own successes. They seemed to self-identify only with whatever was handed them. That is **not** the way of the American mindset.

Perhaps the following story can best explain the liberating way to see life!

When I was fourteen years old my parents were friends with a neighbor who worked for GM and helped design the first Corvette. He was father to a family that was also artistically inclined. In fact, one of his sons was a dedicated artist. When I first got to know that son, he had just completed a striking acrylic painting and was quite proud to show it to me. It was, indeed, a powerful and detailed work of art.

About two weeks later when I returned to their house I noticed that the painting was gone! He had sold it. I asked if he was sad he had to part with something so fine that he had created. He replied, "I don't feel sad about parting with it because the next painting I do will be even better." I knew he meant it. That sincere remark is a wonderful example of liberty-oriented thinking. He was an ambitious young man with a positive attitude who focused on creating his own success. He could have chosen to see the situation quite differently; he could have seen his artwork in a linear zero-sum-game context. Then he might have said, "This is mine, and I am keeping it so you can't have it." Or, he might have said, "I sold my painting and now I feel sad because I lost something that can never be replaced." However, he had the American mindset and was willing to risk his time and his effort in order to create his own special destiny. Many other cultures offer no such risk-for-reward; therefore, they offer no real possibility for earning a better life or a more promising future. Their lives are forever limited, and they are victims of their national system.

There is a special kind of inner influence that takes the form of motivational satisfaction. Although the English language is vastly descriptive, to my knowledge there exists no proper word to describe this kind of motivational satisfaction. It is a mixture of individual spirit, self-pride and effort. The words incentive and enthusiasm come somewhat close, but they still miss the particular essence. However, if we combine enthusiasm with the desire to be productive, we then get something very special. We get a certain kind of personal pride that also involves our industrious self. We could coin a term to describe this adequately, and suggest the term spride. It is a term that is indicative of the American mindset!

We can gain a better understanding of spride by seeing it in action. Let's imagine two climbers who are ready to scale a big mountain. The first climber sees the giant mountain as a personal challenge potentially involving a great deal of risk. He knows that when he reaches the summit, he's going to take some time to deeply savor his personal victory. The second climber, in contrast, is out solely for the opportunity to impress others—to show off.

For the first climber, the crux of the endeavor is the personal challenge itself. He sees the challenge of climbing to the mountain top as a special opportunity to unleash his best. The last thing on his mind is what others might think of him. In fact, he doesn't care if anyone ever knows about his feat. He has spride, unlike our second climber, who may never know the inner satisfaction spride can bring.

We can also see a much different example of spride by looking back in America's relatively not so distant past. Although this example may sound political, it is really about spride in relation to leadership. That is because the right kind of leadership can encourage people to do better than they would ordinarily do. It can convey motivation and induce one's spride. That is because quality leaders recognize that people have valuable essence, and not just physical beings that only need material reinforcement. Let's look at an example of this kind of leadership provoked spride.

I was a teenager during Jimmy Carter's presidency, but I saw how it was a crushing time for both the American spirit and the American economy. There was a unmistakable feeling of hopelessness and disparagement in the air. After years of watching the nation agonize through Carter's presidency people finally got fed up. As a result, in 1980 Ronald Reagan won the presidential election against Carter, taking forty-four states. Americans overwhelmingly elected a very different man as their next president. That refreshing change in leadership produced a profound national confidence, an improvement to America's economy and a more productive public.

Emphasizing American liberty was also one of Reagan's ingredients for success. That was the very element that was missing from Carter's platform. Reagan tapped into America's spirit-for-liberty, and the American people profoundly felt it. It seemed to awaken the American mindset in most everyone, even those in differing political parties.

Both these men were patriots. Carter was a distinguished US naval officer and Governor of Georgia prior to becoming president. However, Carter lacked the ability to convey the grandness of the American mindset whereas Reagan optimistically and authentically radiated it.

As I look back, I can see that Reagan exhibited a grasp of basic America and see how he boldly promoted America using liberty and American strength as a theme. It was more than just nationalism at work. He successfully emphasized the idea of citizen freedom and understood that government, like contemporary human nature, has no regard for spirit, no regard for progress and no regard for the value of liberty.

Of course, the Reagan presidency had its bumps. Nevertheless, that change of leadership ultimately resulted in the creation of more than 15 million jobs for Americans, significant growth in the US economy, and a virtual end to the feared nuclear threat and global bullying of the Soviet Union. Reagan evoked national can-do spride. He left the Presidency by giving us an America that was much stronger and much more stable than it was when he first took office. Some anti-American elements hated Reagan because of his effectiveness. Liberty by its very nature is not for the groupthink and group control crowd.

Throughout the many years that followed, I continued to hear people say that it does not matter whom you vote for because all politicians are the same. The above example demonstrates how wrong that is.

I am reminded of a quote that sums up the lacking state of a society when it is void of spride: "No society can surely be flourishing and happy, of which the far greater part of the members are poor and miserable" (Adam Smith).

Here we saw how America is really more about human energy than it is about matter, and saw how CHN works to undermine that energy. In the next chapter we will see how CHN works mysteriously using other metaphysical tactics.

## CHAPTER FOUR

### CONTROL: ON TRACK TO RULE THE HUMAN RACE

As I further studied the CHN influential network and got more familiar with it, I began to realize how complex it was. For example, I noticed how the CHN network included the workings of a metaphysical accomplice dedicated to fighting all aspects of individual success so I called that accomplice "success resistance".

I further noticed how CHN and success resistance worked in unison as though they were adhering to a plan; a plan that reminded me of a behavioral procedure I learned in grad school called a shaping procedure.

A shaping procedure is a behavioral procedure that is often used to help achieve big goals. For example, a shaping procedure helped America succeed in its first successful manned moon landing in 1969. It used a shaping procedure to produce the highest quality equipment and the best technical know-how. It was used to shape the project into being an ultimate success.

A shaping procedure works by continuously shedding the least effective elements of a project, as it continuously fine-tunes the most effective elements of the project. Another example of using a shaping procedure is the way it can be applied to super-enhance a student's performance. This is done by continuously honing the student's best talent while ignoring whatever he or she does not do particularly well. Some say this was the basic approach that was used on young Tiger Woods's to form him into becoming high caliber golf pro.

Curiously, I began to realize that the contemporary human nature network uses a twisted variation of the shaping procedure: to increase negative results as it decreases positive results. Put another way, contemporary human nature works with success resistance in tandem to increase the negative aspects of society as they decrease the positive aspects of society. In other words, the CHN network uses a reverse shaping procedure.

To further illustrate this, let's look at the way the contemporary human nature network deals with the idea of individual choice. It uses a reverse shaping procedure to reduce the amount of individual choices that exists, as it simultaneously increases the no-choice population. It does this because its equality-for-all agenda needs an ever-growing no-choice sector for it to expend its control. The American mindset sees freedom of choice as a freedom that government has no right to control.

For many individuals, having choices is a wonderful thing. Choices give life an element of excitement while offering options and advantages of all kinds. The more choices we have, the greater the potential for attaining a higher quality happier life. On the other hand, the CHN network wants to eradicate the realm of human choice. Using a reverse shaping procedure is just one of the ways CHN successfully operates. Success resistance eliminates the amount of individual choices as CHN keeps the no-choice population contained, thus leaving only one option left: the last-resort option. That last resort option is actually a do-or-die choice! People can choose to cooperate and thus become just another slave to the CHN network, or they can choose to give up and die.

Still another example of how the CHN network uses its reverse shaping procedure can be seen in how it works on the American economy. It reduces the more prosperous element of American society while increasing the poverty population. Essentially, it works on the economy (and on the idea of financial success), in much the same way it works on the arena of choice: increase the worst economic conditions as it reduces any possibilities for prosperity. That formula gives it unlimited control. Without a decent opportunity oriented economy, people become extremely limited and dependent on whoever is in charge of calling the shots. The humans in charge are really temporary operatives acting unknowingly as an agent of CHN.

CHN also tried to make America the "whipping boy" of the world. One way it went about that was to always compare America in some way to a utopia; a comparison that no other country had to contend with. CHN always managed to overlook the barbaric past behaviors that the non-Western nations committed, while amplifying America's imperfections.

The CHN network transforms success into something immoral and attaches guilt to it. That is because success in an equality-for-all society ideally should not exist. Eliminating success and failure is part of its compelling illusion.

One could ask why America is being singled out when it comes to having to meet absurd standards. That is not a random thing! It is CHN operating with purpose and working towards its designated goal to control humans and curb their individualistic inclinations.

As I continued to examine the contemporary human nature network, I found it also has the ability to selectively apply its power in other ways. For example, it uses its power to recast highly regarded American ideas, especially concepts involving morality, justice and fairness. To CHN, morality and fairness are not virtues or special values; they are merely its tools. Tools it uses to leverage in order to obtain more control. One example of this can be seen by the way it exploits good intentions to gain control.

Many people judge others, to some degree, based on whether they are acting in good faith. People tend to cut some slack to those whose heart appears to be in the right place because having good intentions impresses people even when one does not achieve good results. It is a form of empathy. However, CHN uses the idea of good intentions and empathy solely for self-serving purposes. It has no regard for acting in good faith and no regard for good intentions. It mechanically works to accomplish its one supreme goal, and that goal has nothing to do with achieving a good result and everything to do with control.

Let's look at another example of how the contemporary human nature network worked on a different moral idea.

## Corrupting the Idea of Tolerance

America in the 1970s witnessed a new movement of cultural awareness that can best be described as the tolerance movement. Tolerance quickly became the new buzzword. People latched on to it because accepting racial differences was the virtuous in-thing to do. This righteous idea certainly started out well and good. Soon, however, the contemporary human nature network managed to get involved in the tolerance movement. It modified its original purpose and changed it to something darker. Tolerance went from meaning the acceptance of all people regardless of their racial or ethnic backgrounds, to a capricious form of tolerance that included a tolerance for negative behaviors.

CHN helped turn the wholesome idea of tolerance and the idea of not judging others based on their skin color into a tolerance for undesirable behaviors and low social standards. Again, CHN applied its reverse shaping procedure in order to help lower the general standards of behavior as it worked to reduce the high standards of behavior. For example, it allowed vulgarity to enter popular music, helped usher in a new attitude of acceptance for economic dependency, and helped to destroy the work ethic. It also undermined the American commonsense idea that positive behaviors are worthy of real rewards, not just symbolic rewards.

Earning real rewards through legal individual effort is a basic American behavioral ideal. However, it is an idea that also represents a theme that conflicts with the equality-for-all agenda. Therefore, the CHN network attacks the idea of rewarding incentive-driven self-regulated behavior. It works to selectively restrict people. Furthermore, CHN undermines the fact that men are inherently different than women even in non-physical ways. It undermines the existence of male-based fortitude, masculinity and risk taking as it negates and denies the natural elements of masculine based behaviors. It works towards creating a genderless homogenized equality-for-all utopian society. It even works to treat everyone equal, even when one individual works much harder and accomplishes more than another.

Another technique used by the CHN network is to manipulate that sentiment we refer to as nostalgia. Nostalgia normally conjures up fond memories of one's childhood, thoughts of cherished personal experiences, or memories of a special romantic event. However, contemporary human nature distorts the way nostalgia normally works. It twistedly romanticizes dark periods of past cultures and adds a baseless affection to them so they seem more like a fairy tale, especially when it comes to cultures which practiced harsh citizen repression. It works by perceptively substituting the brutal reality of old restrictive cultures, with a saccharine narrative that inspires a yearning for those terrible times by conveniently leaving out the bad parts of those times. CHN also succeeds particularly well at using this nostalgia-distortion technique when it comes to old socialist regimes like Cuba and Islamic cultures, because they are cultures that are often sensitive to the idea of holy purity and have little regard for individual rights.

Holy purity is a tool that CHN uses very effectively to sway Islamic cultures into accepting perverse theological beliefs. That, in turn, leaves their general population vulnerable to takeover by extremist sociopolitical factions that gain power by professing holy purity as the objective. It is really control. However, CHN even likes the chaos that political extremists bring with them because chaos creates the need for third-party control, and that gives an added opportunity for CHN to become part of that control! We can currently see an example of Islamic extremism penetrating and taking over Middle East societies. They work as temporary expendable agents of CHN and serve at the pleasure of CHN. The extremists ignore human rights and justify the domination of women by suggesting that men have a holy right to treat women as an underclass group in order to control and use them.

One can see a small example of this kind of distorted nostalgia currently taking place in Germany. It is a small but growing idea called Ostalgie—a misplaced fondness for the old regimes in East Germany, Poland, and the Soviet Union. These were actually very harsh times—times when individuals had zero power over their own lives and faced day-to-day tyranny at the hands of the communist leadership. They were times when any expression of individual free-will resulted in the "offender" simply disappearing, never to be seen or heard from again. Although Ostalgie is currently small, it is an idea ripe for growth, thanks to CHN.

Still another example of CHN can be seen by the way it applied its perverse brand of nostalgia to America when it used its power to paint a synthetic portrait of pre-Columbian Native American culture. It helped showcase Native Americans as being representatives of virtue and Mother Nature's selfless protectors. This was another kind of holy purity that took the form of environmental purity. It again used its nostalgia-romanticizing tactic to erroneously contrast the "purely good" indigenous Indians to the "bad" Americans. It worked to taint America's moral roots by making America appear to be a illegitimate nation, while never scrutinizing the moral roots of other countries. That is part of its anti-American strategy. Extreme environmentalism is also an agent of CHN.

American Indians, in fact, were not so pure or as friendly to Mother Nature as they have often been portrayed. For example, we know that they deliberately set fires to burn large territories of forest. They were sometimes fires as large as the area of modern states that were just set in order to clear the land. They also engaged in what is known as the buffalo jump, whereby they deliberately stampeded herds of buffalo, frightening them into running off the edge of a high cliff so that they could then cherry pick through the fallen piles of dead carcasses for prime meat and hides. The point here is not to denigrate American Indians, but rather to demonstrate that no culture is as pure as contemporary human nature chooses to portray them as being.

CHN was determined to taint America's roots and tarnish America's moral standing because America had abundance, and that made it unequal and therefore unfair to community of countries. America's superiority was converted into being a sign of "unfairness". That unfairness was exploited by contemporary human nature in order to give it added support in its war on America, on ethical individualism, on democracy, on liberty and on capitalism. All things it cannot control.

In America, authentic cultural nostalgia can be seen in the paintings of Norman Rockwell. However, the Norman Rockwell image of America does not offer CHN the control it craves, therefore, it delivers a very different kind of controlling idea: American-style political correctness.

Despite its righteous appearance of working for the common good and promoting equal rights; political correctness, diversity, and multiculturalism were all corrupted by CHN. They were modified by contemporary human nature into becoming artificial formats of acceptable behavior designed to limit ethical individualism. It created arbitrary taboos in order to stigmatize those who wish to honestly and logically question or examine them.

One can see how the moral idea of diversity is now being used to promote the vague concept of comprehensive immigration as it undermines the important distinction between citizens and non-citizens. This is just another example of how quasi-moral ideas are specifically leveraged in order to advance CHN's utopian equality-for-all agenda, and to water America down. It leverages subjective morals in order to obscure the value of individual responsibility and eradicate the idea of individual liberty. All individual oriented behavior is its enemy.

Political correctness, diversity and multiculturalism have been converted into orderly artificial protocols which lack respect for the idea of self-determination, and treat adults as though they are all morally inadequate beings. Political correctness, diversity, and multiculturalism have also become ideas fueled by CHN to repress ethical individualism and short-change individual worth.

The political correctness family of ideas is also an example of how CHN again applied its reverse shaping procedure by coercing people into being part of its self-promoting anti-individual elite group, as it reduced the arena of individual thinking.

Another component to the political correctness family is it arbitrary use of social justice. Social justice was also used by Hitler to fuel his campaign of tyranny and boost his control. Real American justice is about law-breaking and due process, not about singling out and persecuting social groups. Whenever you hear the phrase "social justice" think Hitler.

Individualism was being assaulted because it is a self-regulating idea that is not easily controlled by external influences. The political correctness family of influences is merely another stepping-stone towards a non-existent equality-for-all utopian society.

The contemporary human nature network found ways to punish and ridicule America for many years, and eventually succeeded in knocking America off the front of the world stage. It has little regard for America's constitutional framework, especially the parts that favor ethical individualism and individual liberty.

Another example of CHN at work is the subjective way it influences educational institutions. It neglects to teach youngsters about America's generous goodwill contributions, its numerous humanitarian deeds and its success in using democratic free-market capitalism. It also neglects to credit America for using its powerful influence to promote human rights all around the world. This neglect is no accident and not just the result of someone's conscious intentional neglect. It is the invisible force of CHN tampering with twentieth century world history and the way we teach it.

One can look at what recently happened to the educational format known as Common Core. Its original standards started out impressive, but it unfolded into a socio-political pseudo-educational program. It quickly transformed from a being a promising educational endeavor and soon became an odd contemporary human nature version.

Still another interference of CHN can be seen in the way the minimum wage issue is being framed as an issue about fairness. The reality is that our society needs a plateau that transcends school learning and introduces young people to the job world. It is not about living wage jobs, but rather about retaining irreplaceable valuable intermediate level jobs. It worked to remove the learning-work level jobs necessary for young people to acclimate into the real world. That is because those lower-pay transitional jobs go against the equality-for-all utopian State agenda.

CHN especially beats up on America because taking over America is its big prize. If it can do so, it will destroy the global hallmark of ethical individualism and proceed to control the rest of the world with impunity.

In helping to promote comprehensive immigration, it again uses a sweet-sounding misleading half-truth. Comprehensive immigration is used by CHN as a euphemism that really means "comprehensive gutter-level equality-for-all society". That is a poverty society consisting of a subservient population absent of all individual liberties.

The contemporary human nature network also denigrated America and Western culture by attacking free-market capitalism and making it into a bogeyman. After years of thinking about this, I have come to the opinion that defeating capitalism is the crown jewel for CHN. It is fervently against economic freedom and aggressively works to defeat capitalism. CHN is working to replace capitalism with its controlling; equality-based system. That is flimsy system which people do not live very long and their quality of life is similar to that of the prisoners of a 1940s Soviet gulag.

Let's examine CHN in more detail as we look at it in relation to America's political framework.

## CHAPTER FIVE

## AMERICA GOES FROM PROTECTING ITS CITIZENS TO OWNING ITS CITIZENS

As I continued to study contemporary human nature, I came to a frightening realization. In addition to its general controlling propensity, I felt CHN was closing in on completing one of its major missions; to take over and control America. I saw my own basic freedom was in real jeopardy and saw contemporary human nature as being much more than just a theoretical concept; it was a very personal threat. I saw how CHN was gobbling up control and using the United States government to do its heavy lifting. CHN gets into government and turns it into a control oriented entity. Something that is cruel to innocent citizens and stops at nothing to exert control. When CHN gets control, the results become disastrous for the majority of citizens.

CHN and American liberty each uses control. Contemporary human nature uses control to dominate others. America places the crux of control in the hands of the individual citizen so that they can control their own behavior and use that control in their own thoughtful ways.

I think most Americans would agree that America's political process has become overly image based and substance deficient .We accept political claims that represent empty moral ideals. Plus, we vote for candidates who win elections just by mouthing fancy sounding platitudes without ever having to articulate any rational plan of their own. Furthermore, candidates are allowed to win elections merely by characterizing their opponent as evil, while they themselves dodge the critical issues. Then they create political facades to replace reality and build a campaign based on those contrived facades.

CHN infected America's political system and mixed into government. It is conscientiously working to tilt America towards becoming an equality-for-all utopian nation, and it cares nothing about the best interest of the citizens. CHN will only stop only when the majority of voters become sick of being used as political pawns and they decide to use their voting right wisely by demanding more than platitudes and blame-throwing from their politicians. They may be more apt to use their vote as a sword to fight CHN if they become more aware of CHN's control oriented interferences. That is also how this chapter may play a role.

### Dressing down Political Leaders

Politicians sometimes develop compelling campaign personas in order to attract voters. This compelling element is what is often referred to as charisma. They use their charisma to boost their candidacy and woo voters. Unfortunately, charisma isn't much of an asset after a candidate wins office because quality leadership requires nonpolitical problem solving, the ability to deal with complex realities and an understanding of how to create a economically healthy environment. Additionally, it requires leadership skills, know-how and the ability to effectively manage and maintain a well-run government.

America is obviously lacking quality leadership. People are losing trust in government. America should be an economic powerhouse, but it's not.

Many people base their view of politics on what the popular media claims. The problem is that the popular media often subjectively emphasizes the best image of their favorite candidate, their political party or their favorite policy, while especially highlighting the negative aspects of those who oppose their view. The conventional media outlets also re-package reality in order to sway voters because much of the media is infected with the contemporary human nature mindset and collectively help their side win. That, in turn, causes well-meaning citizens to vote for the candidate who appears more appealing on camera. That then leaves the country with a media star in charge, instead of having a competent leader in charge. The people then end up with a leader that has an impressive style, but no intuitive capacity to foresee or account for the consequences to making bad decisions.

Another problematic aspect of politics is its use of word-finagling, glittering ambiguities and deceptive marketing.

Creating convincing slogans is important to both the business world and the world of politics. They both rely on a handy tool we might term half-truth selling. Half-truth selling is a technique used for the sole purpose of marketing something. In politics, it is used to advance an idea, elect a candidate, support a controversial viewpoint or deliver propaganda.

The half-truth marketing technique works by taking a kernel of truth and crafting it into a palatable short, catchy phrase designed to viscerally convince people into believing something other than the whole truth.

CHN also uses the half-truth method to help it sell its own semisecret plan. That is a plan that suggests that morality resides in an equality-for-all utopian society. CHN succeeds at promoting that idea because an equality-for-all society seems to represent the only fair model of life. Although some people may find that particular ideal appealing, they may not realize that it is really just a misleading half-truth. The whole truth of that sweet, moral-sounding equality-for-all ideal is actually something much different than the half-truth suggests. CHN is really working to create a crass gutter-level equality-for-all society, not just an equality-for-all society. When that whole truth is exposed, the equality-for-all idea quickly loses its appeal because people do not want to live in a crass gutter-level society. It is important to be aware and recognize this half-truth deception whenever one hears the word equality thrown into the rhetoric.

Although I was never a political oriented person, I couldn't help but notice something very unusual. I noticed that an important aspect of the American presidency was being mysteriously omitted from all discussion concerning the Obama Presidency. It was glaringly apparent to me that CHN was infecting the way the presidency was being perceived. The media behavior followed a pattern that consisted of preventing blame for America's problems to befall on President Obama. They were problems that legitimately indicated a Presidential deficiency, yet presidential blame was always being diverted in ways that always managed to let the Obama Presidency off the hook. For example, problems concerning America were always blamed on the intransigence within the body of America's politics, or blamed on the divisiveness within Congress. Everyone was avoiding the discussion of presidential blame and they all robotically overlooked the truth of the matter. The truth is that the President of the United States has a built-in fundamental responsibility to solve problems and work with Congress in good faith for the benefit of the public in-spite of political differences. The President is the chief arbiter in charge of ironing out political differences and bringing unity to the nation. Rectifying and mitigating national and political conflicts is the duty of every Presidency! This entire factor was conveniently removed from all discourse, thanks to CHN.

The President of the United States is also, in no small measure, responsible for the public mood. He controls the power of the "bully pulpit". That gives him the unique power to assure the citizenry that they are secure, that he is an inclusive leader and to convince the American public that they are being governed competently. Furthermore, the president is also responsible for forging agreements with Congress and fortifying good relations with America's allies. Oddly, this subset of presidential responsibilities was not being mentioned. This was largely the result of the Obama Presidency being given a pass by CHN.

Although I took American history in the tenth grade, much of it did not sink in at that time because it seemed irrelevant to my life. However, that was then and now is now. Recently, I felt it was the time for me to get more reacquainted with the real America, so I proceeded to closely study America by focusing on grasping the gist and salience of America, rather than just the usual textbook portrayals of it. As a result of that effort, I inadvertently uncovered a dirty little secret about America that gets drowned out by the noise of politics. America is really the embodiment of the constitution.

Additionally, I began to see the many countries around the world that were experiencing violent rebellions and chaos within their borders, and I realized that there was one particular weakness that they all had in common. They lacked a firmly rooted, procedural charter that organized their nation and articulated the relationship between citizens and their government. Plus they had nothing to prevent their country from becoming a monarchy or their leaders from becoming tyrannical kings. All these factors highlighted to me the value that America's constitution and its authentic rules of justice provides us Americans. Social justice, religious justice and economic justice all turn into proxy items to serve CHN.

As I further studied America, I learned many other novel features about it. Furthermore, I also found myself inadvertently rediscovering the splendor of basic America, and freshly realized how wondrous America really is. Let's take the constitution for example.

The United States Constitution has stood as an active, authoritative national document for well over two hundred years, and is the structural glue preventing America from falling apart. I found a particular grandness in the way it allows the majority of citizens to decide elections while still providing for individual liberties. To those with the American mindset, the constitution is a national scripture. It gives Americans something big and real to believe in.

As I looked at America's Constitution, it found it interesting in more ways than one. One particular reason that it fascinated me was because it seemed to have been designed with the fear of selfish control firmly in mind, and I have been studying selfish control for decades. I also looked at the constitution in other ways and found that although it is strictly a government charter, I learned how its existence is indirectly responsible for many other protocols and procedural formats. For example, although property rights exist in many other countries, America's property rights often include the right to a land's underground minerals and the resources that lay below the surface of the property. This one factor alone is responsible for other implications, legalities and opportunities that go along with property ownership. Additionally, I discovered other important uncommon American characteristics. Some had to do with banking regulations, intellectual and real property laws, insurance rules, bankruptcy laws, tax structures, and many other investment related regulations and laws. However, some of America's novel characteristics involved long established American values and culturally embedded ideas such as the specific legal age of adulthood, the rights of next of kin, parental and legal guardian responsibilities and family law, just to mention some. Another important value derived characteristic can be found at the way America's criminal system is designed. It puts the onus of proof on the accuser and State, and the presumption of innocence is given to the criminally charged. They are not guilty unless formally found guilty in a court of law and are given the right of due process. This approach to justice is a reflection of an American value based cultural priority which believes that it is better to let a guilty person go free than to wrongly convict an innocent person. American justice is designed to automatically and completely give the benefit of the doubt to the side of individual liberty. Some cultures find this approach ludicrous and don't really care about convicting innocent people.

Some basic American procedures and legalities came from English common law while some originated from Ancient Greece, Ancient Rome and the Roman Empire. The writings of great thinkers like John Locke also had substantial influence in the construction of the nation of America. However, some of America's characteristics and features stemmed from basic values with distinct religious roots. The Talmud is one example of a philosophical and religious inspirational source. The Talmud considered "giving" both a solemn obligation and a way that G-D rewards generous individuals. Furthermore, it was the source that led to the formality of using one's signature as a means to confirming financial transactions, agreements and legal documents. It also contributed to our modern ideas of justice fairness and proper business conduct, because honesty in business was considered by the Talmud to be a divinely expected individual duty. Some Biblical ideas were also brought into the Plymouth Colony Capital Laws of New England in the 1600's to later be used as a foundation for some of our most basic current laws.

Another example of a long-time established American value can be found in the formality of taking an oath of office or swearing to tell the truth when testifying in a court of law. Still other examples include child labor laws, parental obligations and that children are provided an education.

Of course there are literally hundreds of great books and sources that delve into America's cultural origins and root values. The point is that the reason these cultural values are worth mentioning here is because the basic American way of life is not the result of arbitrary relativism. Rather, much of America is based on particular values that were (and are) imbedded into its very fabric. CHN does not like to compete for control. It wants wheel its control whenever it needs and does not want anything standing in its way. It only works within a single linear dimension. It always fights traditional national values, constitutional issues and religion because they all have non-linear conditions that oppose the unconditional equality-for-all goal.

However, there is still another elemental aspect to American value system that CHN totally ignores. That is the element known as "good faith dealings". It is basically the idea that people should deal with others by always applying good faith intensions and always in honest mutually understandable ways.

Standing back, one can see yet a much broader American feature that relates to its vast vision of citizen rights. While many other countries base their notion of citizens' rights only on what government expressly permits, America's vision of rights are centered on the premise that individual rights are undefined and basically unlimited. In other words, adult citizens are automatically guaranteed the right to make their own decisions, and to initiate or engage in any unstructured original behaviors they wish to (provided they are within the law). This makes America unique in the way it offers its citizens an open realm of individual liberties not subject to governmental restrictions.

On the other hand, CHN again uses its signature reverse shaping procedure and attacks or intimidates everyone that does not conform to its equality-for-all illusionary goal (whether it is legal or not), while it subsidizes everyone else. It broadens the conforming population by subsidizing them as it punishes the self-achievers. Thus, it takes a giant step towards achieving its illusionary equality-for-all society in a way that lowers everyone's standard of living. No one wins.

America also has an especially cherished and distinct subset of rights that are part of the Constitution. They delineate some of the specific things that government expressly cannot do. It is that venerable collection of the first ten amendments of the Constitution known as the Bill of Rights, a document that describes some essential citizen liberties in relation to the limitations of government. However, to CHN, the Bill of Rights is nothing but a meaningless hindrance and a minor roadblock in its path to acquiring more control. As a result, CHN has launched an assault on the Bill of Rights. It will try anything to increase its own control, including the total disregard for individual rights. It even manipulates the meaning of rights. That is why we shall now attempt to take a closer look at the concept of American rights.

A few years ago I saw a news story showcasing a young, twenty-something woman holding a rather unusual protest sign that read, "Utilities Are a Right!" She was fighting for the idea that home utilities are rights because they are so vital for human life. Hence, she was suggesting that items such as water, heating oil, and electricity should be available for free, just as people are allowed to breathe free air. That was all I needed to hear in order to realize that many Americans see America as something different than what it really is. They also expect the government to have a responsibility it cannot adequately fulfill, principally when it comes to giving. These misconceptions have grown to become a profound contributor to America's great political divide and the basis of many misunderstandings that CHN had a hand in establishing.

The American mindset sees individual behavior as being important to opportunity. Opportunity requires human effort whereas gifts are received non-contingently. It also thinks that everyone willing to work should be given the opportunity to engage in individual economic mobility and the opportunity to increase their earning power.

CHN has also done a remarkable job of muddying the waters between assumption and reality, especially when it comes to defining America and its role. It judges all behaviors by using convenient arbitrary group metrics without factoring in America's constitutional realities. CHN also operates much like the behavior specialist we discussed in Chapter Three that acted by manipulating the lab-rat using reward, punishment, and negative reinforcement, all for his own controlling interest. Even more so, and in much the same way, contemporary human nature uses America as its Skinner box and treats the American citizens as lab rats. That is precisely the kind of scenario that America was designed to prevent!

Because of the mass confusion about national rights and about what America really is, I felt we should critically visit some common misunderstandings and perhaps shed some new light on this subject. Furthermore, I thought it was important to attempt to call attention to some of the basic relevant (but seldom discussed) American tenets and principles, such as the real meaning of American rights. I thought my background in the study of control could help bring a novel aspect into the discourse. Let's look at that story about utility rights again in a different way.

The young woman fighting for free utilities made an excellent fundamental point. People do need utilities to stay alive. Without getting into too many sad details, hers was quite a story of the heartbreak that she and her family had endured while trying desperately to keep their home electricity and heat turned on. I was surprised at how well she articulated her case based on a well-founded, if gut-wrenching, moral argument. Her argument, however, also presented the opportunity to see the meaning of rights in a genuinely American way.

If we look at the issue of rights purely from a rational point of view, logic might suggest that something cannot honestly be considered a genuine right if it gives to one citizen by taking away from another citizen. Forcibly taking finances or property from some Americans in order to give them to others is not a basic American application of justice in addition to its being a dishonest use of rights. The American mindset sees giving as a personal voluntary act. When force is applied to giving, the scenario smashes the authentic concept of rights and enters into the arena of social responsibility. Although the same moral and ethical argument still applies, there is a big difference in those two arenas. That is why taxes should be enacted carefully with respect to the constitutional framework.

America has one group of citizens who think it is up to the federal government to provide material necessities to citizens, and has another group of Americans that view rights through a basic American lens. They have the American mindset we spoke of, and do not believe that satisfying the material necessities of citizens is the job of the federal government. Rather, they feel that doling out money and services to citizens reinforces dependency, plays politics with taxpayer money and is not constitutionally kosher. They also believe that "government giving" is not a question of morality, and not a real answer to our humanitarian problems. Furthermore, they believe government should not be a money broker involved in arbitrarily redistributing the people's coffers. They further believe that just throwing money at problems is worse than sincerely trying to solve them.

Although CHN suggests that the mere discussion of many humanitarian issues is heartless and racist, the American mindset sees these issues as being really about constitutional order and honesty. They also see rights as natural freedoms, not insincere government gifts. In either case, this is an issue that should be thoughtfully examined and rationally confronted.

One can easily justify federal agencies such as the Center for Disease Control, national defense, national parks, and food safety being some examples of legitimate government responsibilities and appropriate federal services. However, CHN has taken the "government responsibility" issue beyond the bounds of traditional American civility. We can now see our own government, along with its rapacious agencies, becoming tyranny.

I think it is now fair to say that the centralized Washington government model is failing us. Furthermore it appears to be poised and empowered to trap us all into a life of lowly obedience, low quality living and political bullying. However, this fate can be peacefully prevented by simply turning to the Constitution for the answer to the problem.

Due to the incredible growth and power of the federal government, one can easily forget that it was really the creation of the original 13 sovereign Colonies; Colonies that became officially recognized as States in the late half of the 1700's.

Before writing this work, I vaguely recalled once reading the Tenth Amendment many years back, so I then decided to look at it again. However, this second time I looked at it through the lens of control and saw it quite differently. I saw how it contained an important underlying rationale that went far beyond its literal meaning and I felt that it is worth sharing. First let's look at the Tenth Amendment.

## The Tenth Amendment:

The powers not delegated to the United States by the Constitution, nor prohibited by it to the States, are reserved to the States respectively, or to the people. (that's it!)

The Tenth Amendment was accepted into the Constitution because the states wanted specific written protection from big government—and they got it. The Tenth Amendment (if enforced) takes some of the bloated central control out of Washington, DC, and puts more responsibility on the States and on the people themselves. The underlying reason this amendment is important (and the reason that it needs to be taken seriously) is because it conforms to America's natural structural design: layered government. Like the more familiar American separation of powers structure involving the three branches of government, layered government also protects American citizens from centralized control and balances governmental powers. Now is the time for both concepts to be recognized and utilized.

As I looked closer at the Tenth Amendment, I came to the belief that the basic American layered structure may well hold the secret to defeating much of contemporary human nature's destructive control. Let's look at the Tenth Amendment as it relates to layered government.

America is composed of States, districts, counties, municipalities, and a variety of other jurisdictions of all shapes and sizes. These "layers" each offer their own brand of possibilities that can help pick up some slack resulting from the trimming of our enormous centralized government. That could enable inner America to utilize its layered resources more effectively while empowering the States. A federal downsize project could create a governmental structure that is more responsive to citizen needs.

Although implementing the Tenth Amendment may result in States developing their own contemporary human nature problems, federal downsizing could be done wisely and would deflate some of the counter-productive contemporary human nature control.

Furthermore, it also seems reasonable to assume that if well-planned; applying the concept of a citizen- participation oriented layered government would bring the federal government down to a size that makes more sense. With the federal government less involved, the local governmental layers could be geared to work more in concert with each other and concentrate on actually serving citizens. That could result in better solutions to problems, such as the problem that was mentioned in the utility rights story. It would also remove much of the political acrimony that now exists because most people would develop a more personal relationship with their government. One can think of it as the government practicing diversity when it comes to using the various levels of government that exists. Government powers could be sectioned accordingly and organized intelligently while still retaining individual choice and liberty.

Another advantage to establishing a more layer oriented government is that it would unleash more flexibility in the States forcing them to be more resourceful and more innovative, instead of just being federal adjuncts. Among many other advantages, each State could help design specialized vocational and work learning programs that are demographically aligned with their own unique needs and natural assets. They could work closer with their counties, and more effectively with the businesses, corporations and educational institutions within their State's borders.

The federal government could be winnowed down so that it was preforming only those things that it legitimately does well while still maintaining prudent safeguards. For example, The Civil Rights Act of 1964 that outlawed discrimination based on race, religion, sex or national origin could still be federally enforced and also applied to all levels of government. That would supply America with an additional governmental separation of power platform and a more power balanced nation.

Life in a more downsized federal government environment would consist of a more in-touch public because things like the local police, school boards, local taxing and zoning authorizes would become more relevant to daily life and thus would require citizen participation on all levels. It would also open up an opportunity to design a supplemental system where tax credit can be earned through community work because less taxes would be necessary.

Thanks to our modern age of internet accessibility and the visibility exposure it provides, rational technology based systems could be designed in ways that force States and other government entities to be transparent, accountable and open to public scrutiny. That would encourage government entities to take the high ground and guard against cronyism and citizen abuse; because those would become more problematic. Ethical standards would be expected and enforced by citizen watchdogs, local elected representatives, State representatives and finally federal representatives. There could be a form of layered oversight where each localized sector and each government layer would be watching each other in order to protect the vulnerable citizens, avoid possible corruption and prevent the more powerful from trampling on the rest of us. Although America is a free-market capitalistic nation, local government and communities can augment the capitalistic system by being secondary support resources to buck up public safety and help provide other services.

Another focus of attention would be to help equip individuals with economically valuable trade skills so the localities don't become lifelong reformatories that don't provide residence a way to work themselves out.

States, mayors, city councils and communities could network, share and model good ideas while having the opportunity to showcase their accomplishments. They would all be in a position to tailor ideas in ways that work best for their own jurisdictional populations. Citizens will need to collaborate in good faith and use the ability to collectively synthesize and implement good ideas. Workable ideas will be continuously fine-tuned into becoming better ideas. Companies would contract with localities to set up and run energy micro grids to supply electricity to residencies, hospitals and residential care facilities. Localizing America could unleash a powerful sleeping layer of America; the individual humanity brotherhood layer that works with the original wise design of America.

Unlike much of Europe and other parts of the world, America has the flexibility and has millions of citizens with the American mindset who are capable of helping design a more local geared nation. Here is where that American mindset can demonstrate the value that cooperative thinking and intellectual capital has over economic capital.

Another important attribute of the American mindset is its attitude when it comes to responding to an honest challenge. That is an attitude commonly referred to as the "can-do" attitude. It will be essential to have that attitude in order to successfully decentralize the federal government. That will be especially needed when CHN uses scare tactics and aims its influential powers to deter and demoralize any efforts towards independence. It will fight like hell.

Unlike the usual top-down federal government approach to dealing with matters, the localization of America project can focus on individual empowering bottom-up approaches to address community deficiencies and facilitate local employment opportunities. It can be designed to reinforce positive doers, job creators and the idea of self-reliance. It can also be designed to help fill the critical gaps that capitalism cannot fill.

Building a well-organized local empowered America should ultimately produce stronger communities, more working citizens, and a better take-home pay-to-expense ratio. Plus, America will be made up of community involvement where personal interactions made from sincerity and compassion will be some of the currency used fund local service projects, and people will turn to one another in order to help fill government assistance voids. It need not be just an arena for the desperate; it could also be a citizen emancipation and social idea that crosses economic lines. A landscape that presents a host of opportunities for everyone well-intended to pitch-in, express their own helpful talents, apply their American mindset and vent their own input in novel ways.

A variety of local exchanges, goods-and-services co-ops, peer-teams to help with citizen needs and the creation of innovative local food sources with delivery chains may emerge.

After all, Americans are considered to be the most productive workers in the world. Many however are unfortunately idle, but have skills and spirit that beg to be constructively used.

All this will have significant legal implications that would have to be addressed by our politicians, such as liability issues.

Another potential positive by-product of localizing America would be its need for vigilant responsible handling of tax dollars. It would force national and local government budgets too be kept efficient, more locally accountable and publically transparent. Localizing America will not replace government; it will augment government with non-government citizen involvement, and would reduce the unnecessary power of centralized government as it increases the liberty and quality of life for everyday Americans. Of course, this localization endeavor would need a cooperative President along with a Congress that was also on-board with the idea. Litigation and regulation reforms would need to be applied conditionally. Plus, it would also need robust widespread public support. My sense is that America may be well getting to that point.

CHN will also be at work too. It will subjectively amplify fear provoking news stories as it attempts to obscure the real value to localizing America. It will feel threatened by this independence effort and it will produce deceptive smokescreens, diversions and employ tactics of all kinds.

We spoke about liberation oriented thinking in Chapter Three. A localizing America project will also take good thinking individuals willing to break the shackles of the shallow reflexive mind. Exercising intellectual freedom is also an authentic part of the American mindset.

Though not explicitly mentioned in the Bill of Rights, critical-evaluative thinking is an individual right by virtue of the fact that it is an exercise that represents a logical extension of the First Amendment. Many cultures forbid alternative points of view or impose blasphemy laws prohibiting it; however, the American mindset makes good use of critical-evaluative thinking for a variety of reasons, all of which are protected by the Bill of Rights.

The American mindset believes information and knowledge should be honestly considered and shared, not used as articles for control or manipulation. CHN hates those who oppose big central government so it casts them as evil. Although it becomes more radical as it desperately tries to protect its control, it is no match for the American mindset (especially when the American mindset is ready for its wrath).

Despite what its name may imply, critical thinking is not necessarily just about being critical of something. It also means to challenge or consider differing ideas, thoughts, ideologies, and assertions. Critical thinking is essential to education, information processing, research and progress of all kinds. It also is part of America's greatest entitlements; the entitlement to free-debate. Furthermore, the determination to hunt for truth and the decency to allow others to be heard are both traits of the American mindset.

Although the American mindset finds creative ways to tactfully approach difficult subjects, personal views can still be very divisive, especially when each person is reading off of a different page. I recall many years ago overhearing two college roommates argue. One argued how the other roommate did not see the light, while the other argued how the other one did not see the light bill. Now that was an interesting difference of opinion. I guess even the arena of critical-evaluative thinking has its limits.

The theater of critical-evaluative thinking can also be used as a corrective aid to help reinstitute a new course of action when things go wrong as they often do.

Critical-evaluative thinking is raised to an even higher level and really liberated when it is forced to confront certain kinds of questions. I am referring here to a particular breed of question that we can call the 'limitless question'. These are questions that catapult the focus of attention beyond the visceral domain, and beyond all conventional thinking. It's when the mind enters the unstructured visionary realm and novel ideas are then hatched.

Here are a few samples of limitless questions: "Is there an alternative to viewing this situation only in terms of either/or?" "What exactly is it we are trying to accomplish?" Injecting questions such as these into a dialogue keeps the focus directed to the topic's substance and that leads to new possibilities for problem solving and progress. Limitless questions also prompt intuitive insights.

The following is another example of a good limitless question that can be used to generate original ideas: "Can we talk about how to improve the future instead of just complaining about the past?" Another example of a limitless question is, "Can we talk about what we should do instead of what we shouldn't do?"

Thought-provoking limitless questions stifle CHN and force consciousness into a mental productive zone. Here is a good example of a limitless question that could have come from the American mindset: "How can we solve this issue in a way that still preserves individual choice?"

## The Bottom Line

I guess we have come to a point where the metaphysical meets the political world. America's is being challenged. This meeting of two very different paradigms is not a friendly one, and it was not new to the original architects of the constitution.

"The natural progress of things is for liberty to yield and government to gain

ground." - Thomas Jefferson

As a result of my supplemental education that focused on America's relation to the hidden forces of selfish control, I learned some important lessons. I not only learned that America can defang and defeat CHN, I also learned how America can best achieve its great potential. Its great potential can best be achieved not by expanding the meaning of rights, not by changing America's limited government format and not by making America fancier. After over five decades of living here as an American citizen, I learned that America is a rather amazing progressive constitutional republic whose real potential can best be attained by electing effective leaders who have more than just good intensions. I believe that means voting for candidates who unequivocally express the American mindset; produce a plan for building a opportunity-filled growth economy, stand for policies that address the global competitive market and only those who are unambiguously committed to working towards a stronger America; an America that is a model for the world.

Furthermore, I learned that although contemporary human nature is determined to defeat American individualism and liberty, Americans may not so easily become its victims.

I hope this book has shown how we have a winnable fight on our hands.

## CONCLUSION

Throughout the course of this work, we have exposed how contemporary human nature saps energy from individuals in order to increase its control. Furthermore, we have shown how this sinister force can wear away at the most successful element of a society as well as thwart ethical individualism, independence, liberty, capitalism and America. (Anything that includes individual desire, individual decision or individual input).

We have also shown how this metaphysical force that quietly works as a methodical network of deceptive insincere influences. It also delivers polarizing imagery, perverse group-oriented ideas, and bogus messages into the consciousness. It is the mysterious self-serving force supporting big government and supporting the popular media, and it must be actively fought because it will not magically go away. Worse yet, it works towards an illusionary goal. Fortunately, the American political arena provides a solution because it is a free-market capitalistic economy with justice oriented oversight, a three-branch constitutional republic, a multi-layered system and a free-marketplace of ideas. Furthermore, we have also shown how individuals can work within the system to empower themselves.

Today's America needs all the help it can get in order to overcome its tired polarizing and implacable political story lines. This book should help change the face of the conventional political story by introducing the reader to the non-human control element behind much of our politics, and helps awaken all to the best parts of America's culture and potential. That helps shift us from just seeing our problems in a political context. Now, hopefully, we can see the real enemy and real danger confronting us; C-O-N-T-R-O-L.

## The Bill of Rights

Amendment I

Congress shall make no law respecting an establishment of religion, or prohibiting the free exercise thereof; or abridging the freedom of speech, or of the press; or the right of the people peaceably to assemble, and to petition the government for a redress of grievances.

Amendment II

A well-regulated militia being necessary to the security of a free State, the right of the people to keep and bear arms shall not be infringed.

Amendment III

No soldier shall, in time of peace, be quartered in any house without the consent of the owner, nor in time of war, but in a manner to be prescribed by law.

Amendment IV

The right of the people to be secure in their persons, houses, papers, and effects, against unreasonable searches and seizures, shall not be violated, and no warrants shall issue but upon probable cause, supported by oath or affirmation, and particularly describing the place to be searched, and the persons or things to be seized.

Amendment V

No person shall be held to answer for a capital, or otherwise infamous crime, unless on a presentment or indictment of a grand jury, except in cases arising in the land or naval forces, or in the militia, when in actual service in time of war or public danger; nor shall any person be subject for the same offense to be twice put in jeopardy of life or limb; nor shall be compelled in any criminal case to be a witness against himself, nor be deprived of life, liberty, or property, without due process of law; nor shall private property be taken for public use without just compensation.

## Amendment VI

In all criminal prosecutions, the accused shall enjoy the right to a speedy and public trial, by an impartial jury of the State and district wherein the crime shall have been committed, which district shall have been previously ascertained by law, and to be informed of the nature and cause of the accusation; to be confronted with the witnesses against him; to have compulsory process for obtaining witnesses in his favor, and to have the assistance of counsel for his defense.

## Amendment VII

In suits at common law, where the value in controversy shall exceed twenty dollars, the right of trial by jury shall be preserved, and no fact tried by a jury shall be otherwise reexamined in any court of the United States, than according to the rules of the common law.

## Amendment VIII

Excessive bail shall not be required, nor excessive fines imposed, nor cruel and unusual punishments inflicted.

## Amendment IX

The enumeration in the Constitution, of certain rights, shall not be construed to deny or disparage others retained by the people.

## Amendment X

The powers not delegated to the United States by the Constitution, nor prohibited by it to the States, are reserved to the States respectively, or to the people.

America is truly a gift to its citizens and a beacon of freedom and prosperity for the rest of the world. However, in the end it is only as good as we make it.

Thank you for allowing me to share my thoughts and ideas! I am honored that you read my book!

Your comments are always welcome.

DonFloyd@Reagan.com

www.ingramcontent.com/pod-product-compliance
Lightning Source LLC
Chambersburg PA
CBHW061516040426
42450CB00008B/1649